This Coloring Book Belongs To:

....

....

GRAFFITI

COLORING BOOK

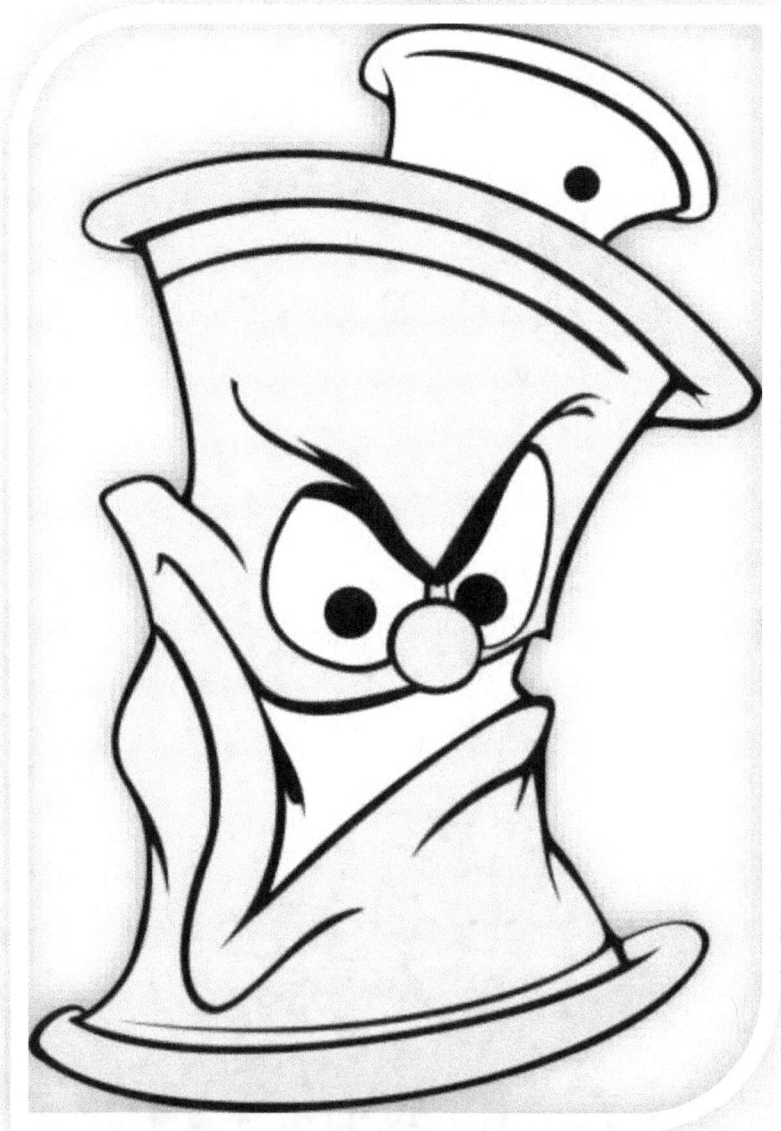

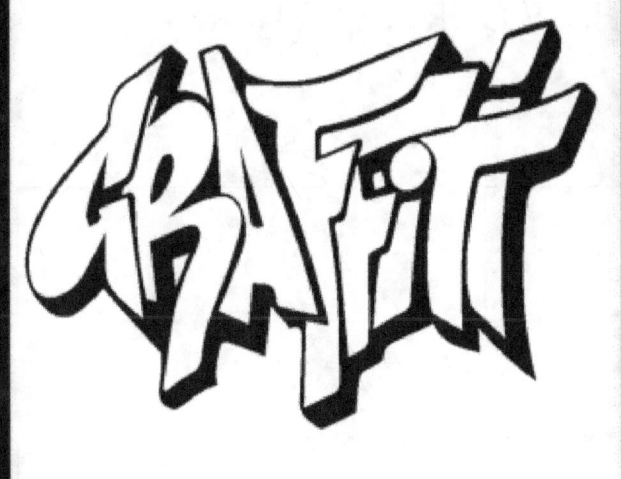

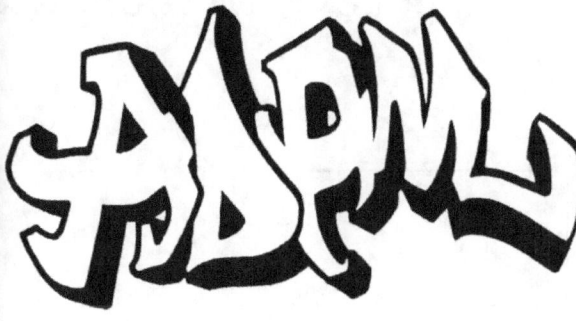

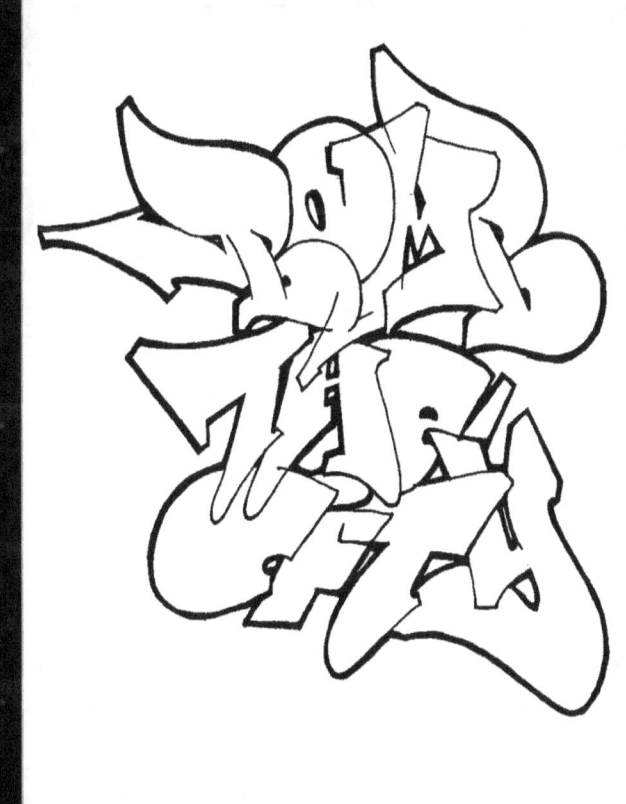

TEST COLOR PAGE

CHECK HOW YOUR COLORS SHOW OUR PAPER HERE

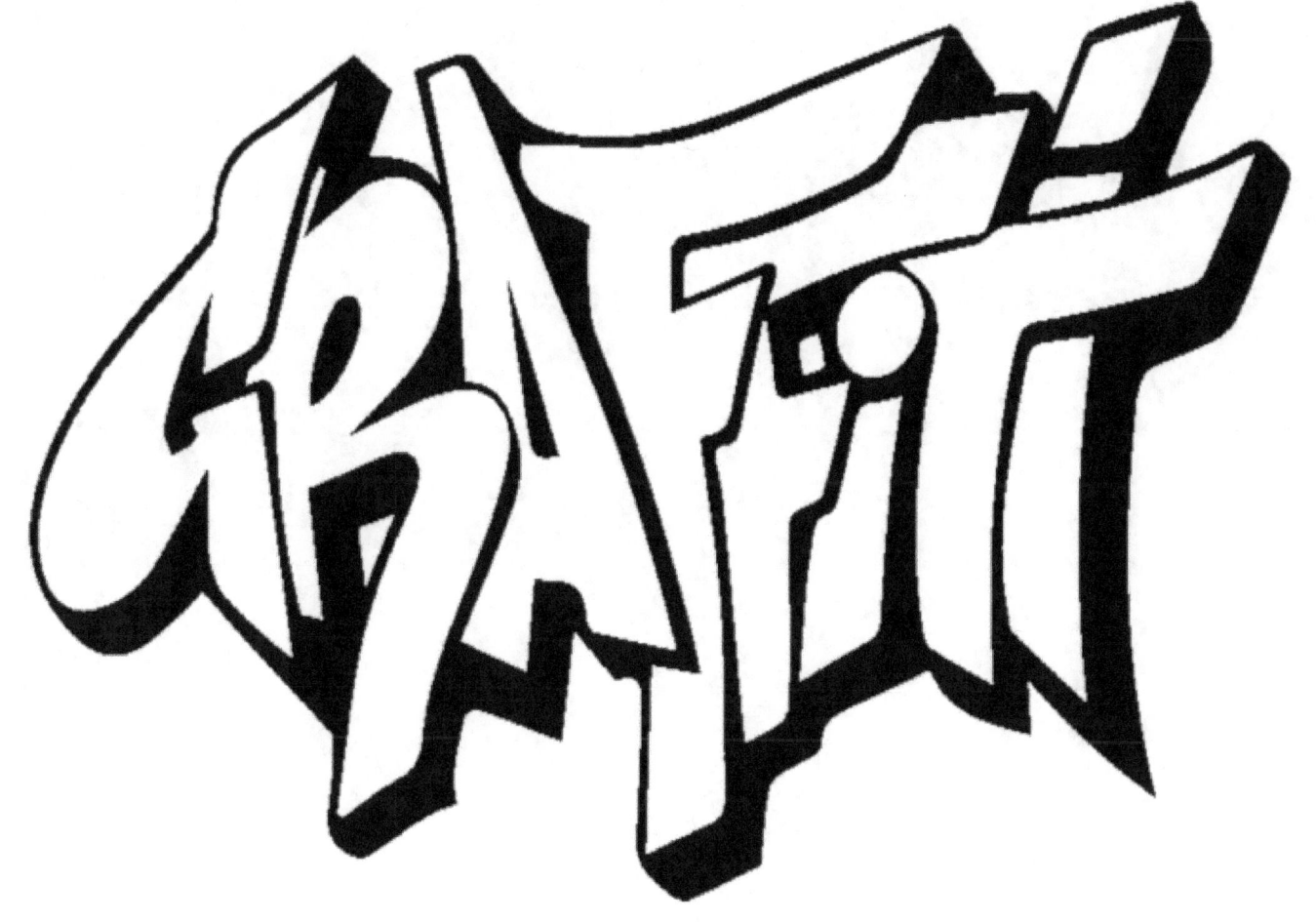

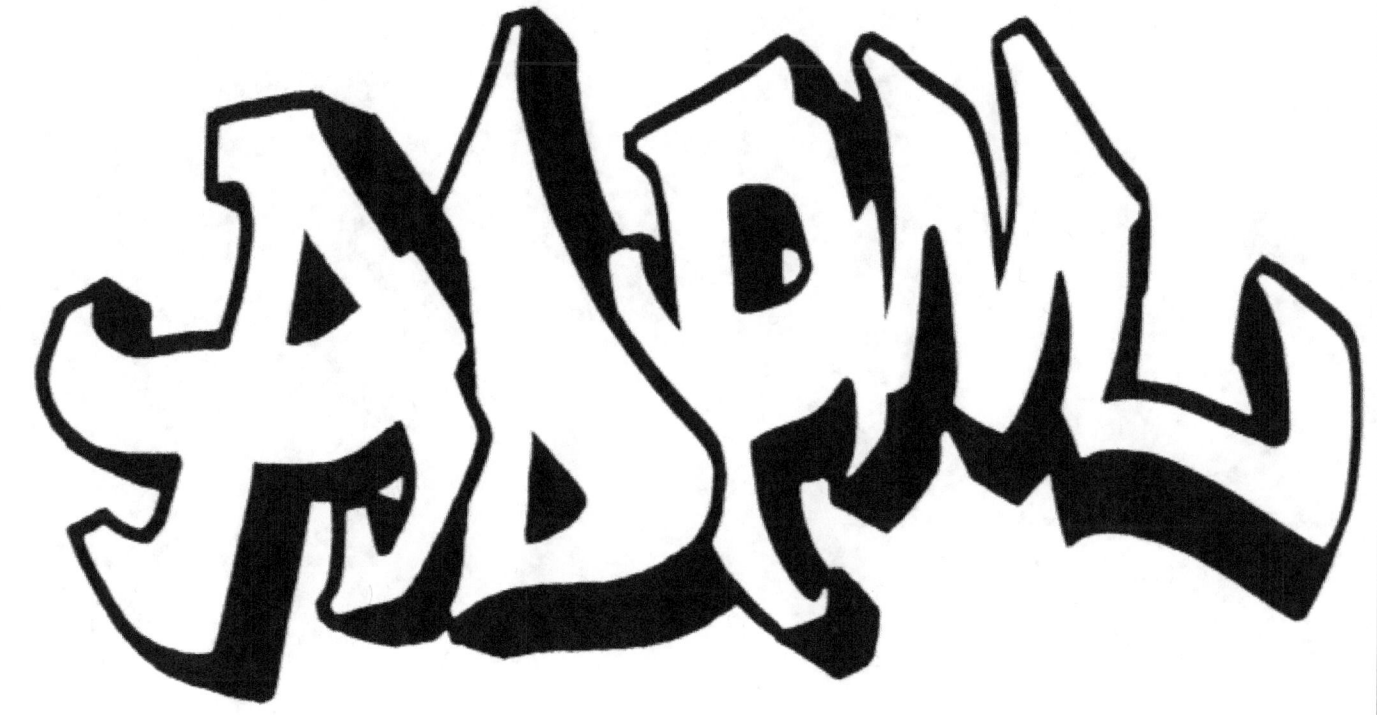

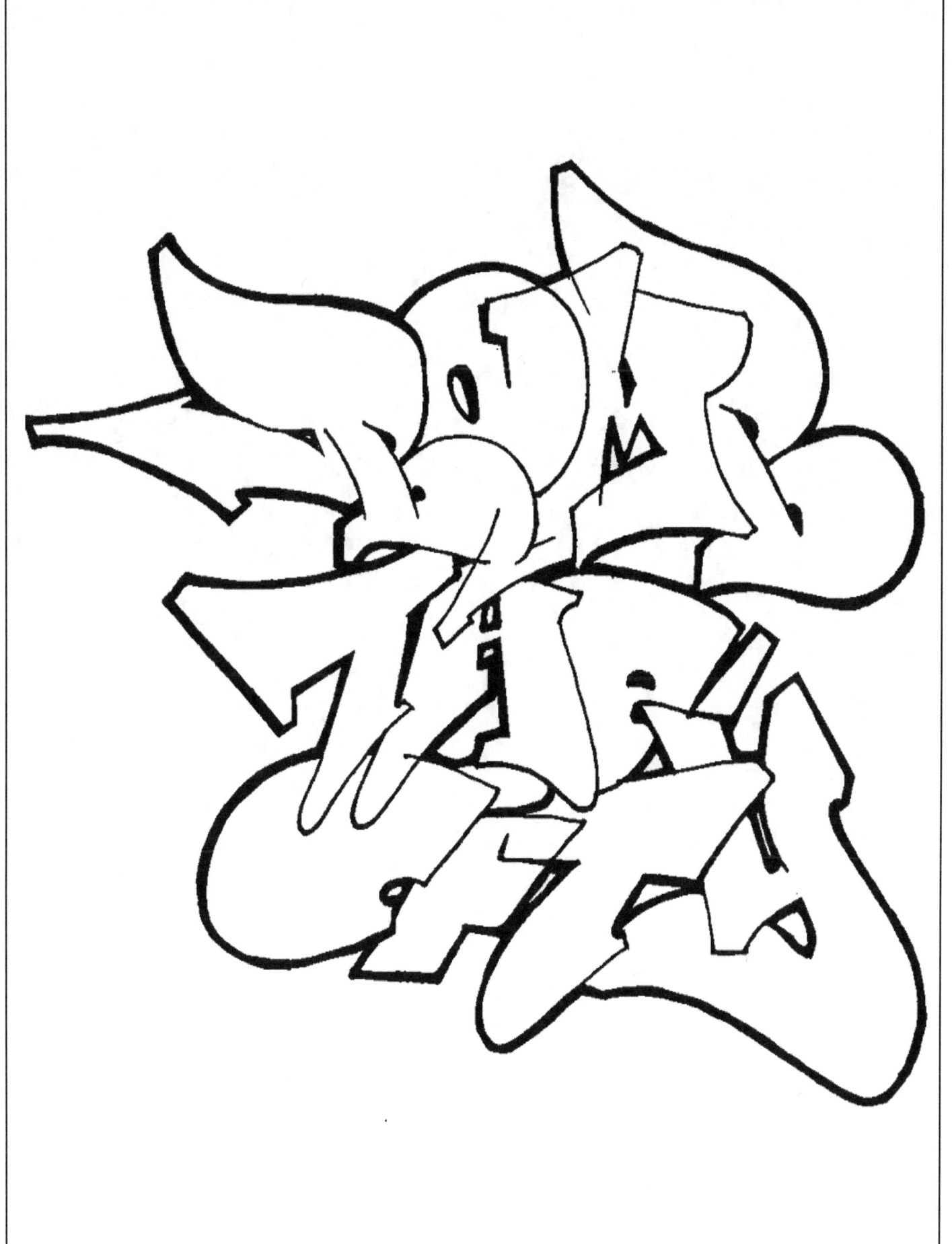

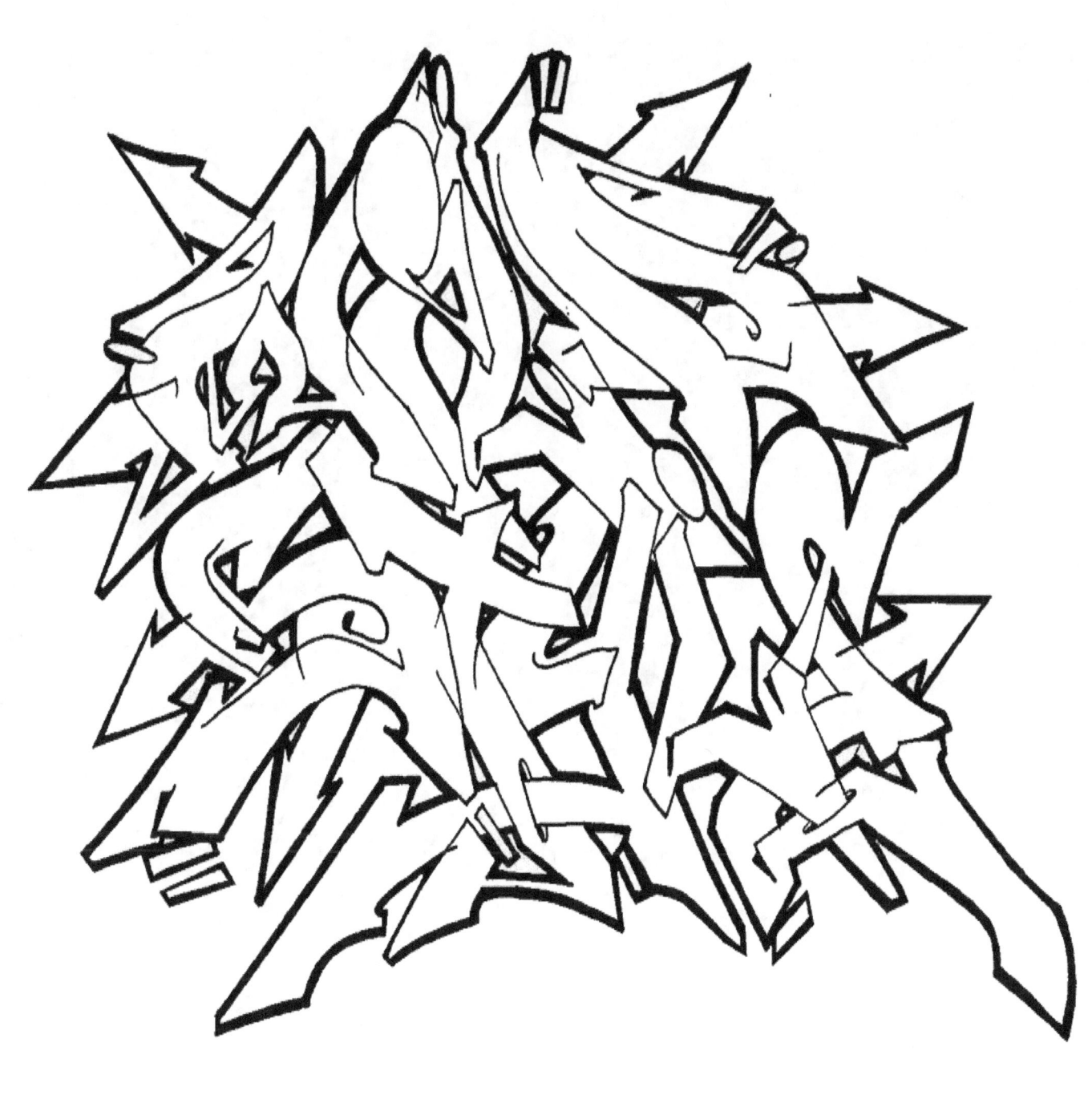

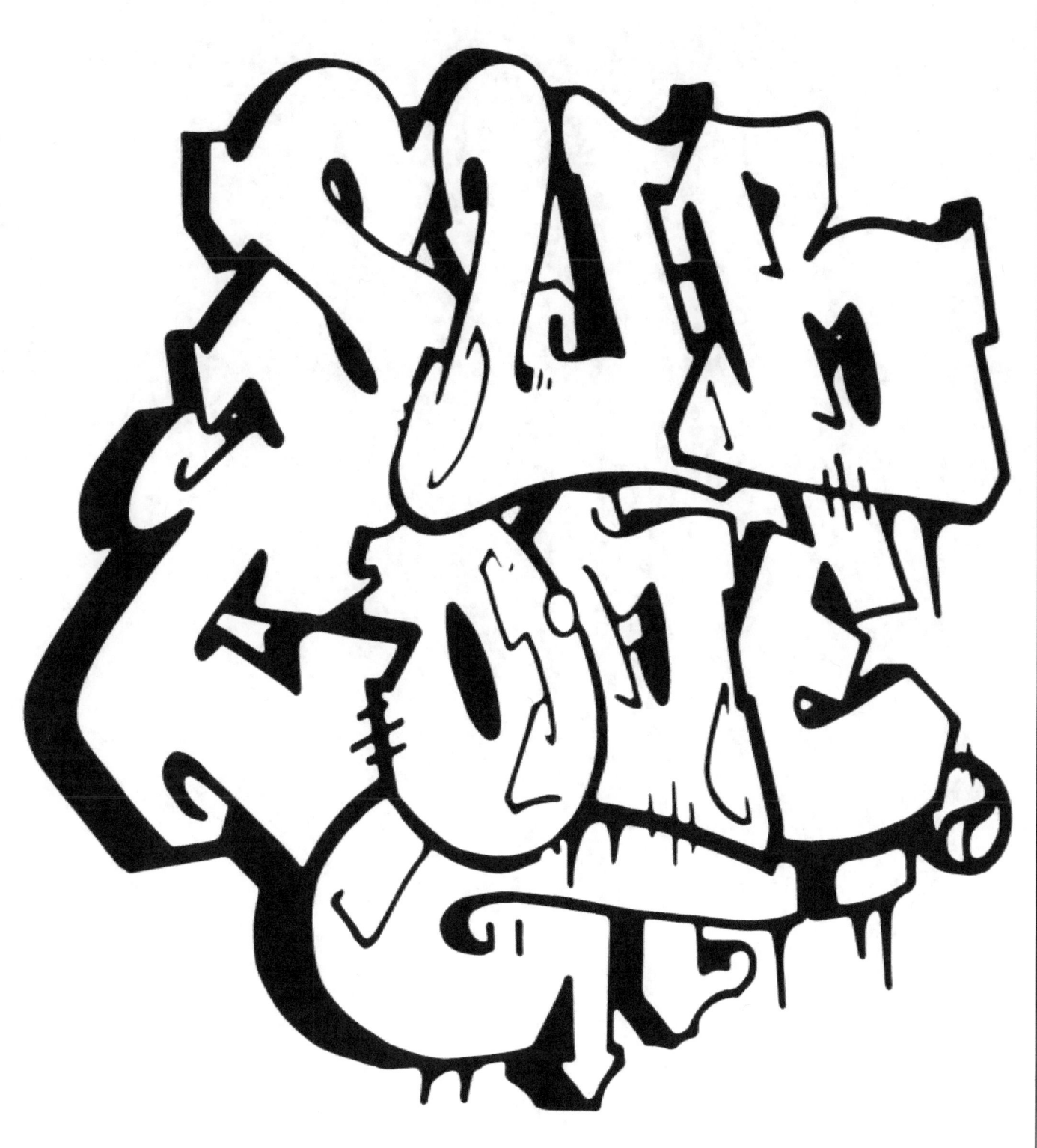

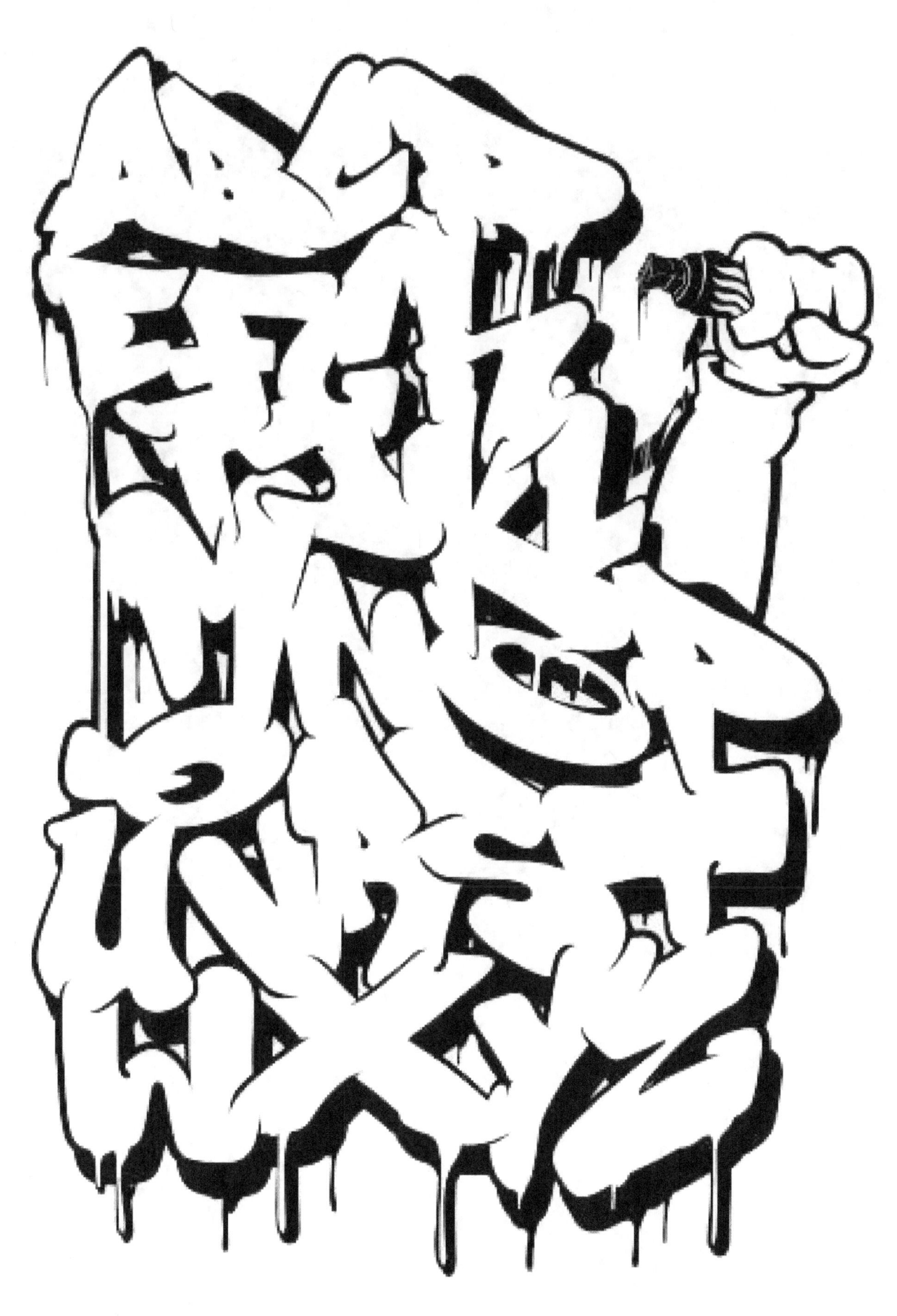

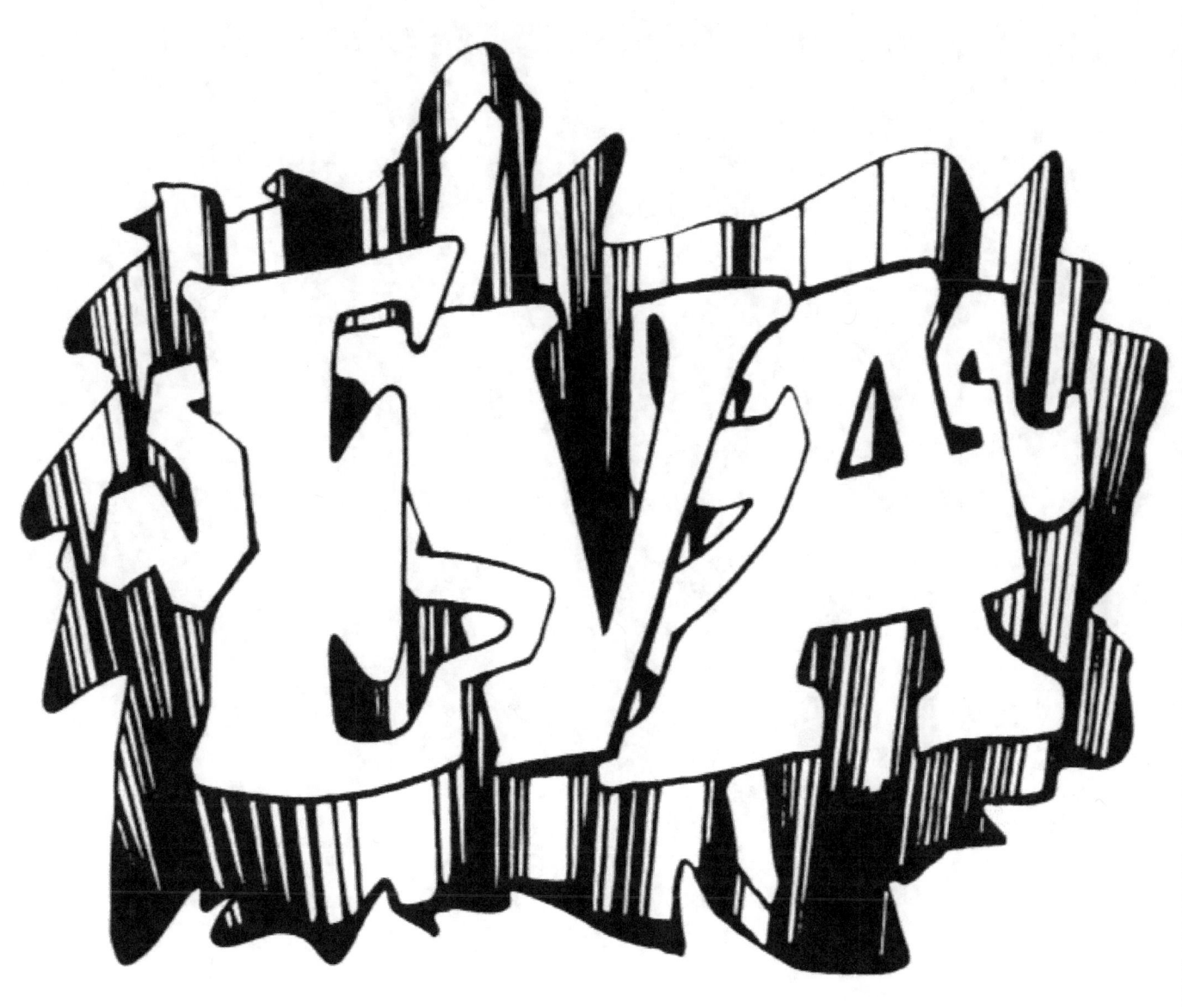

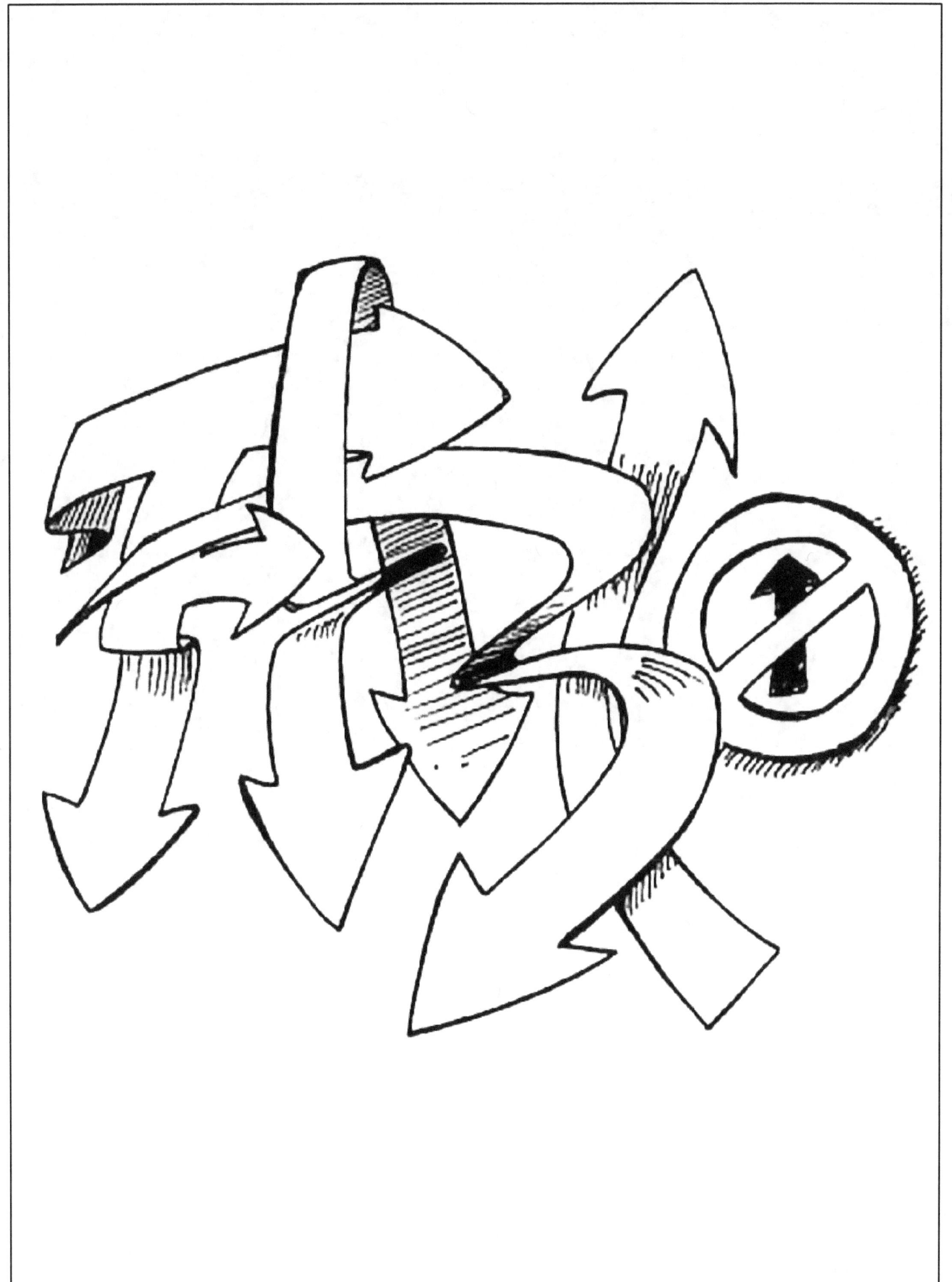

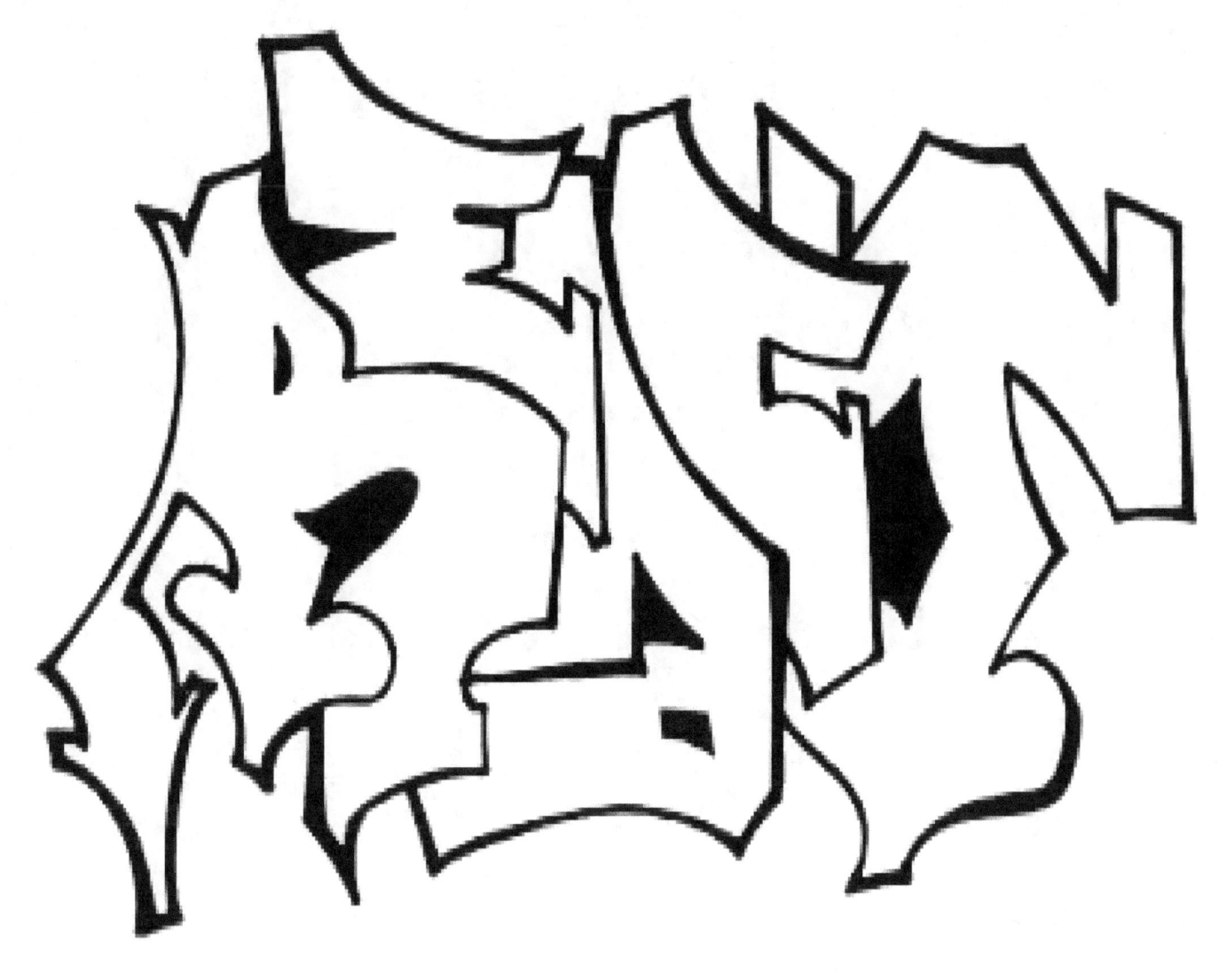

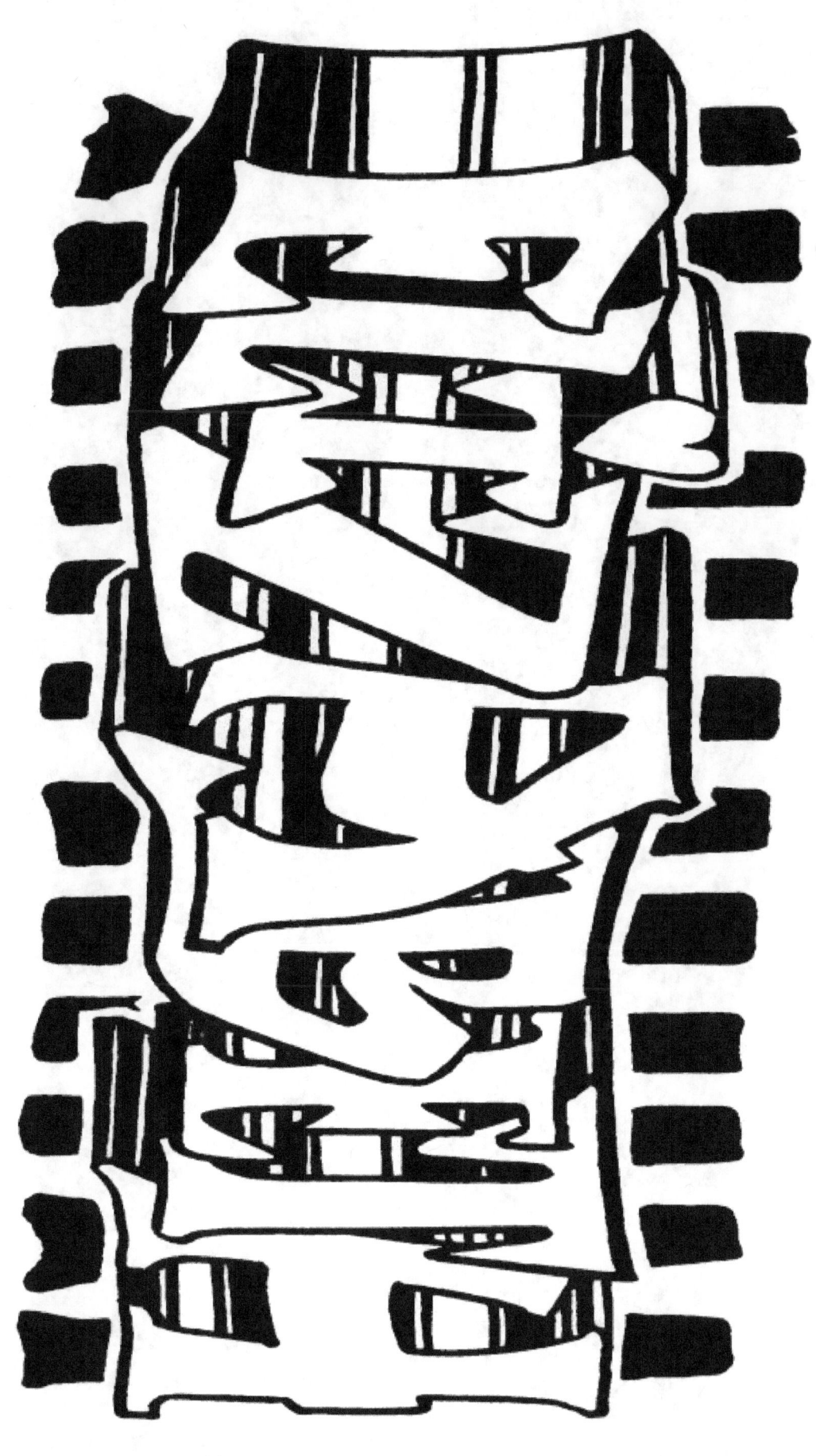

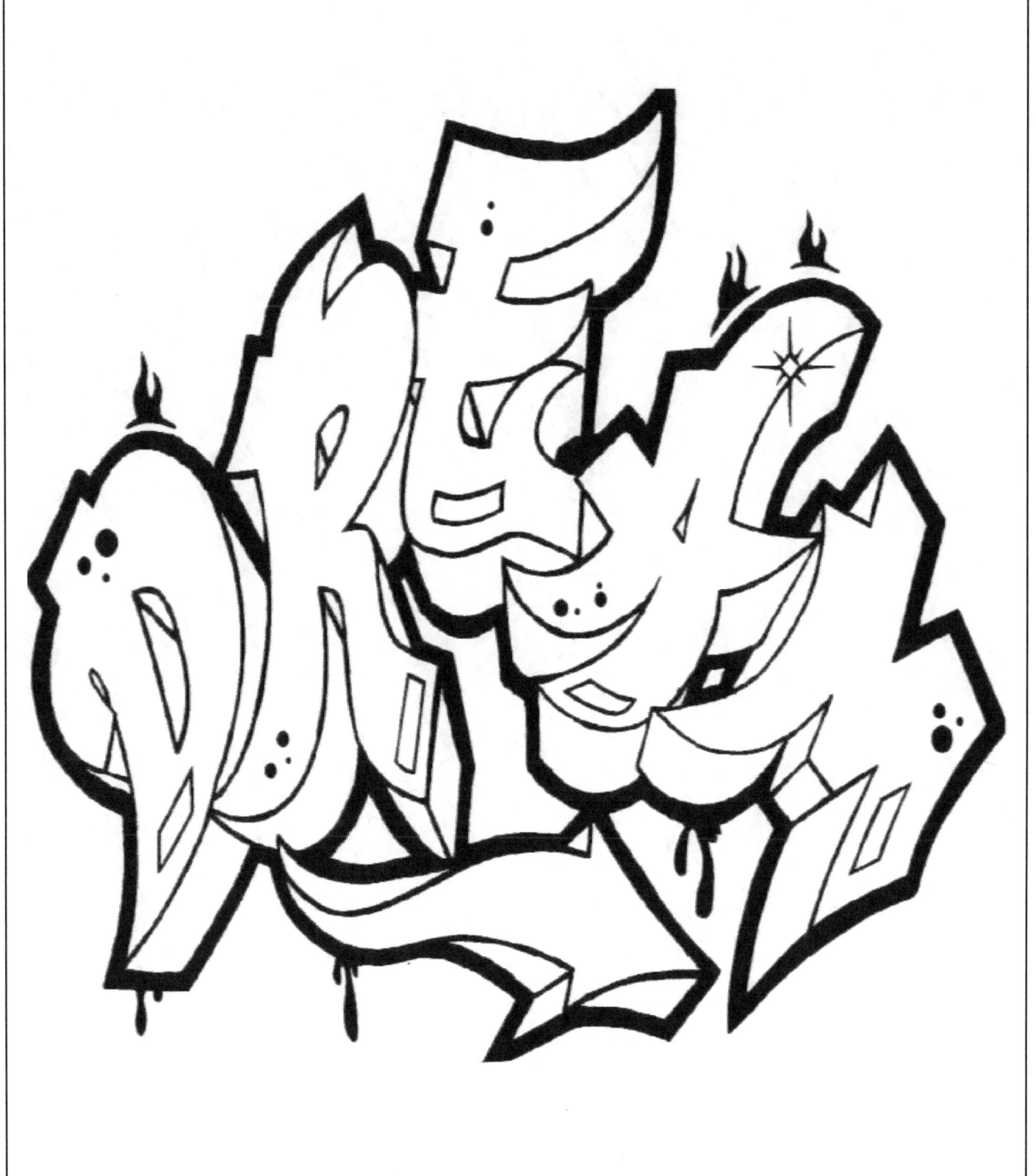

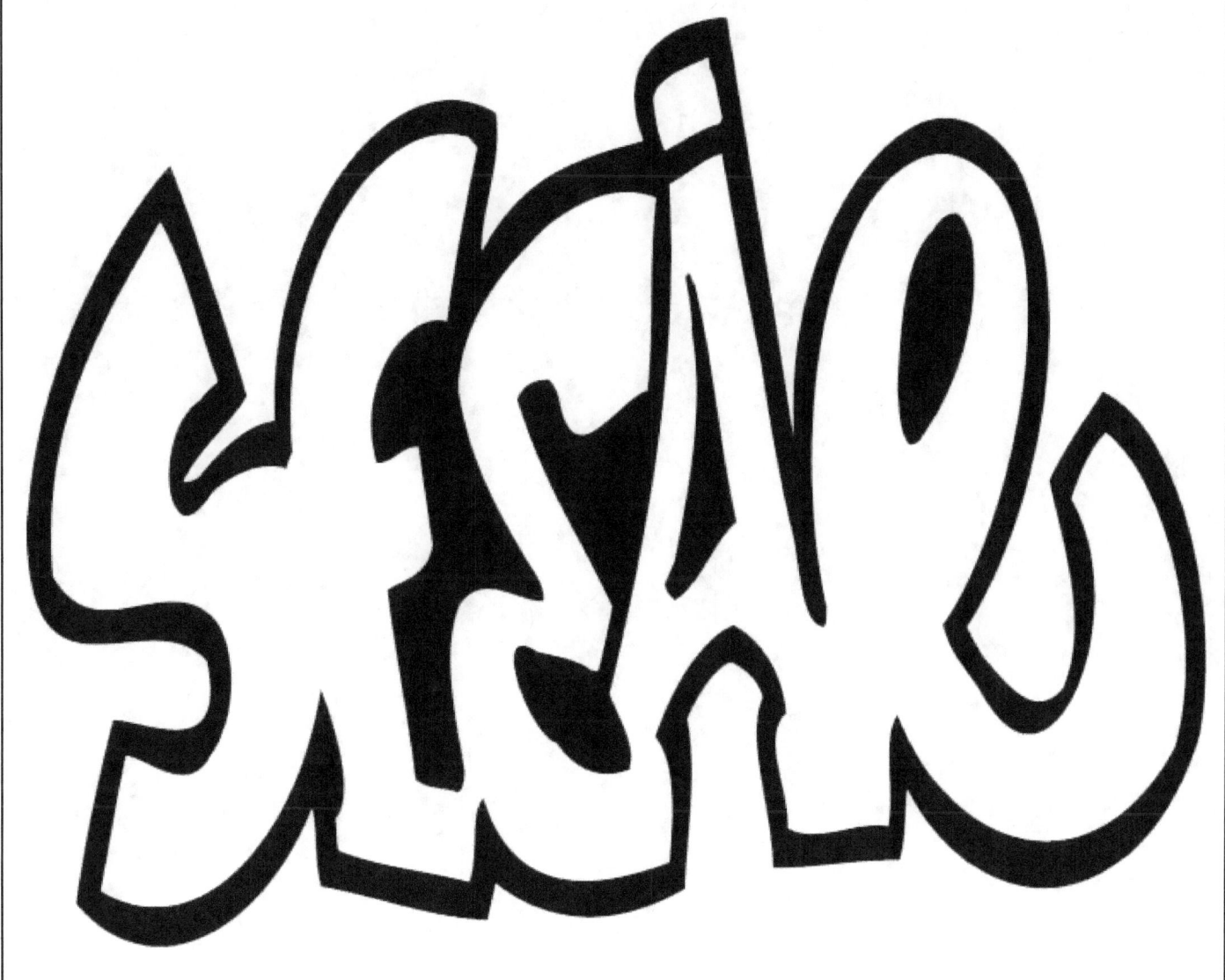

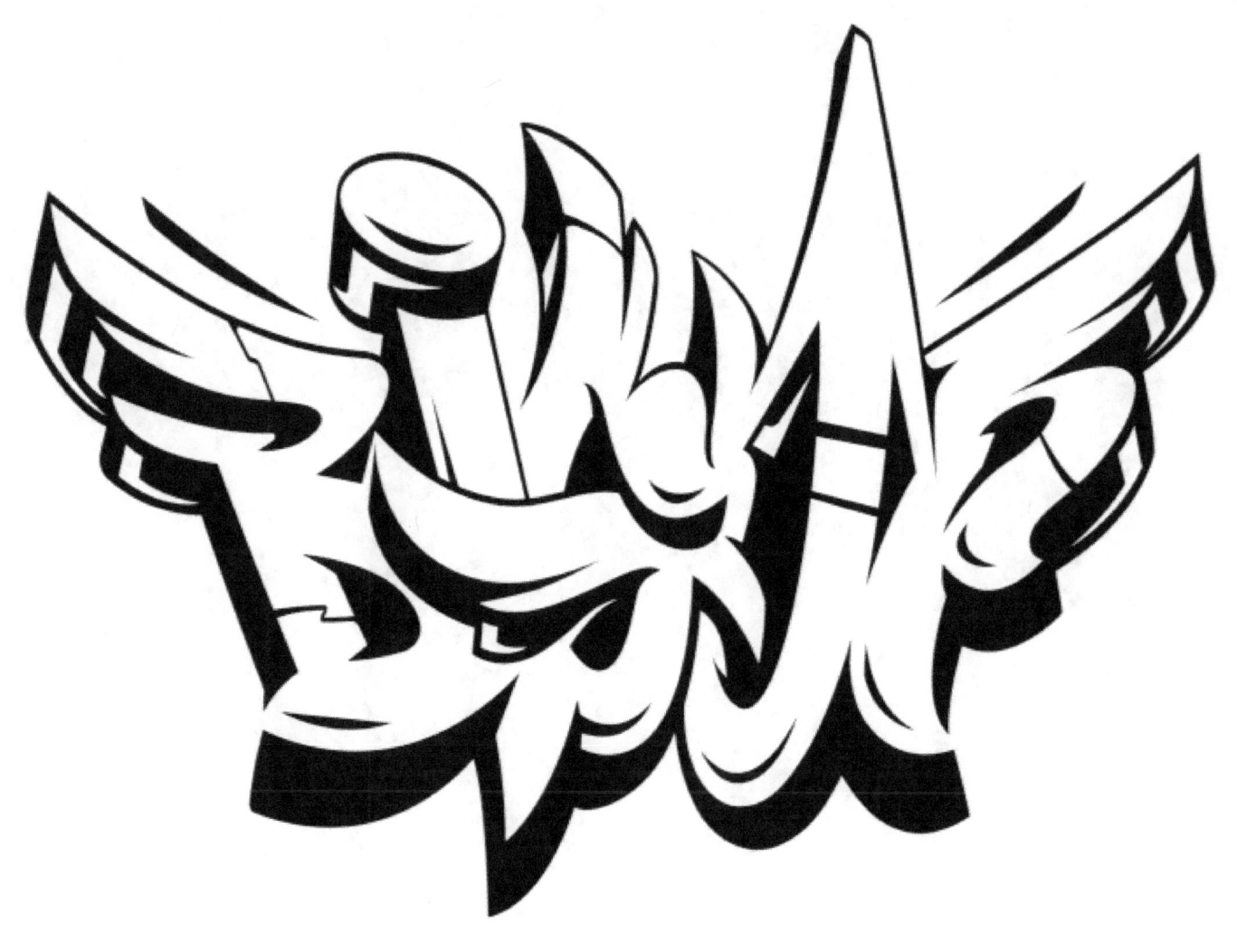

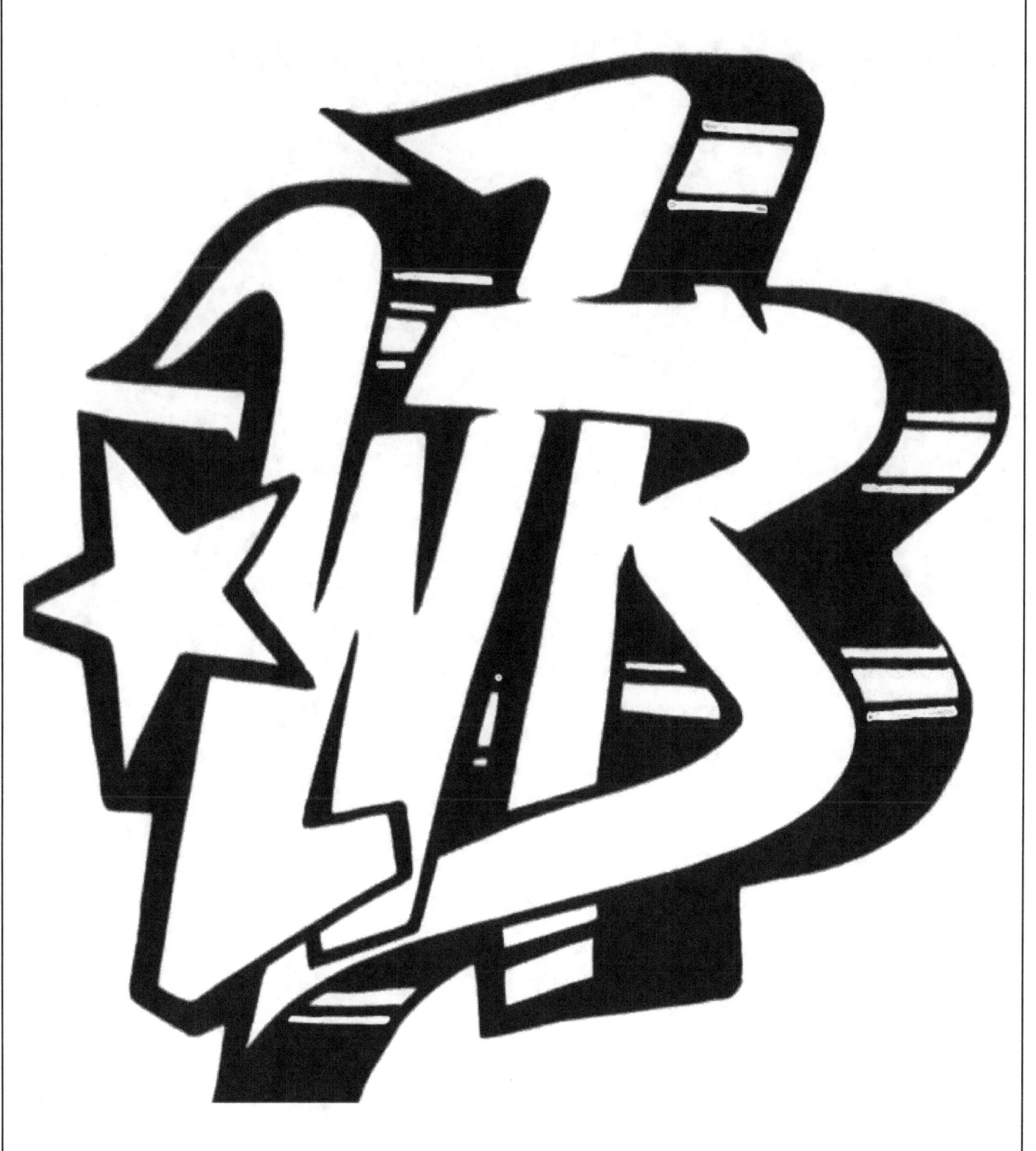

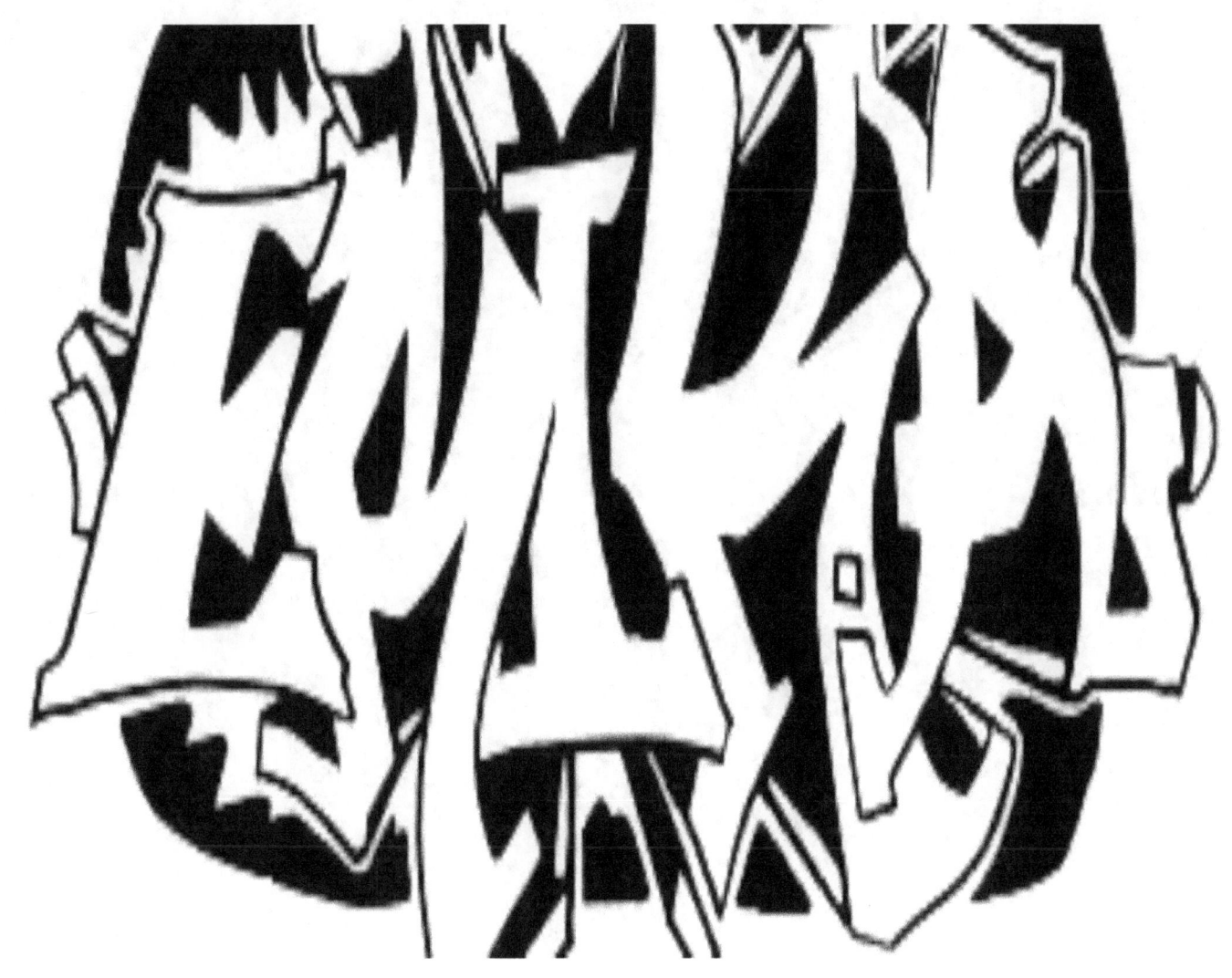

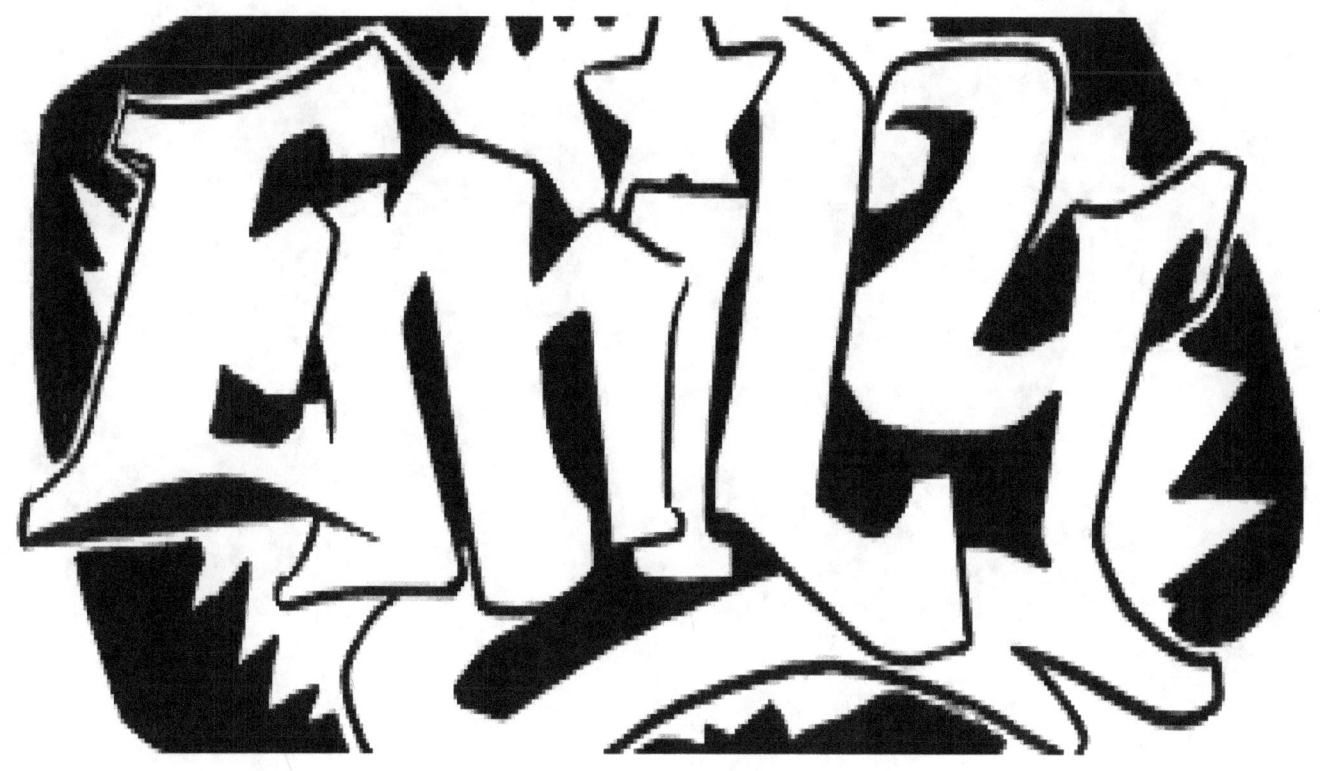

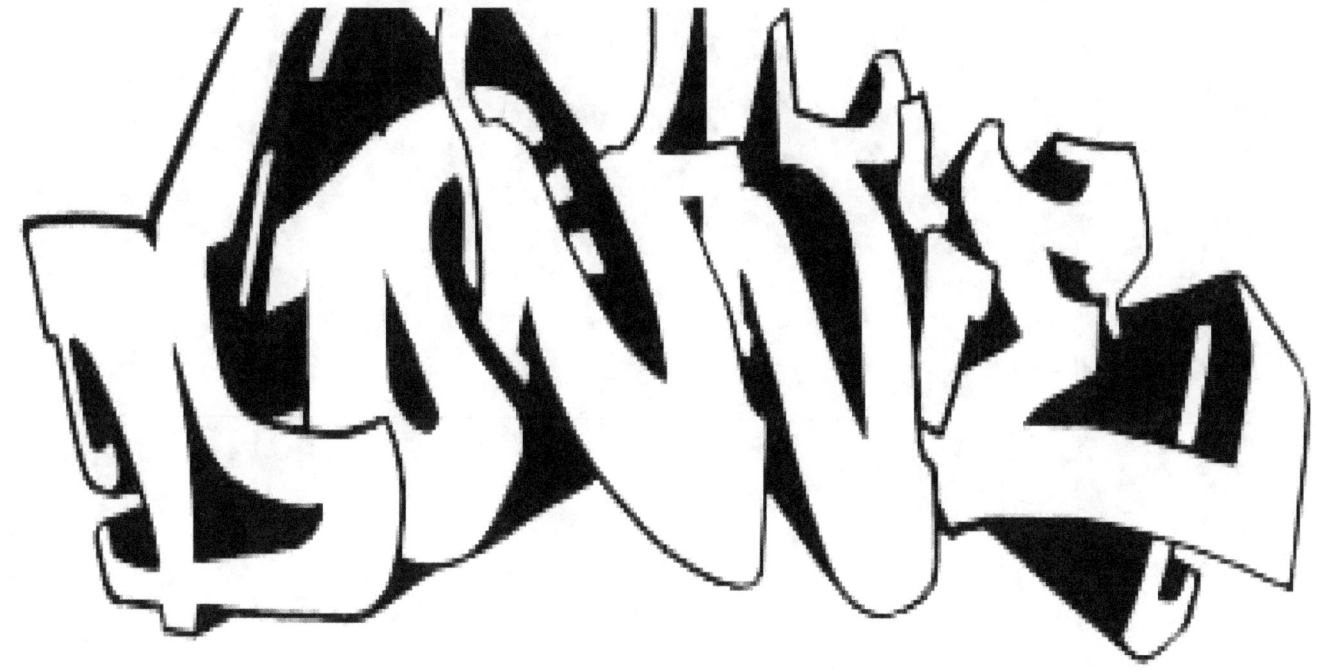

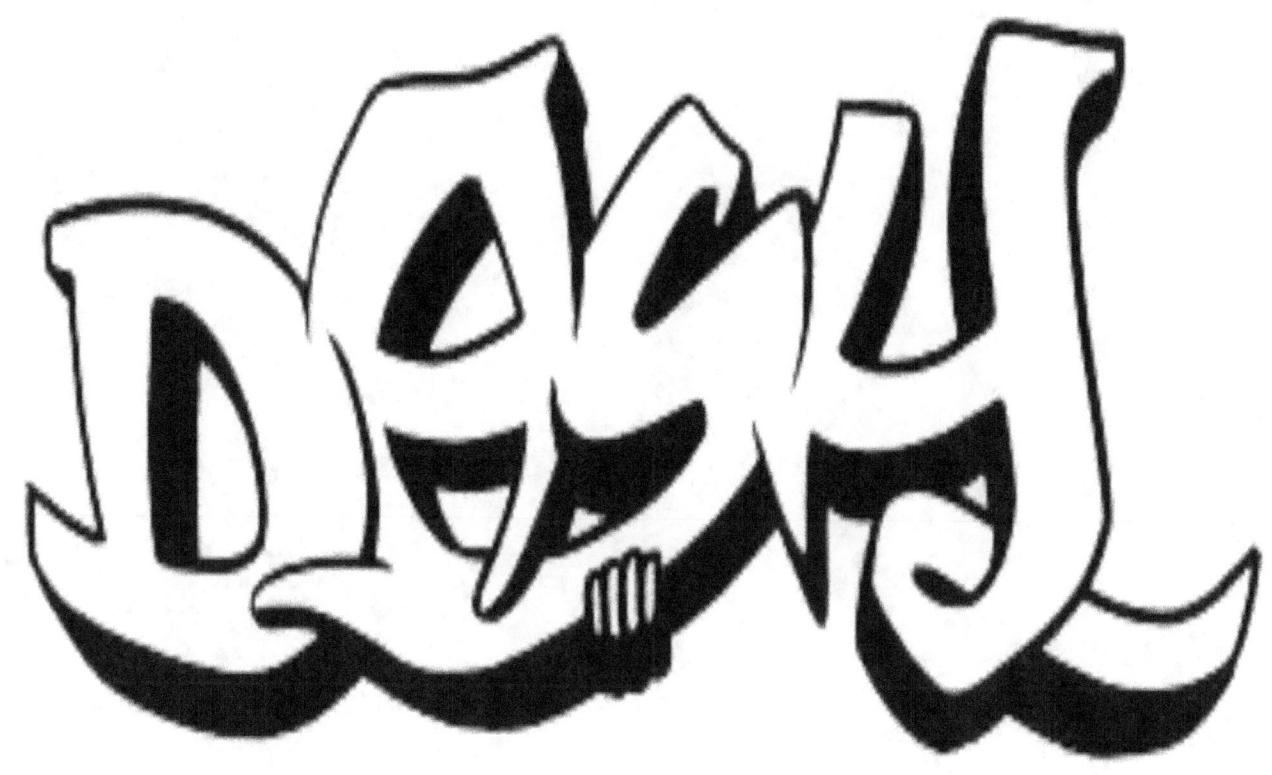

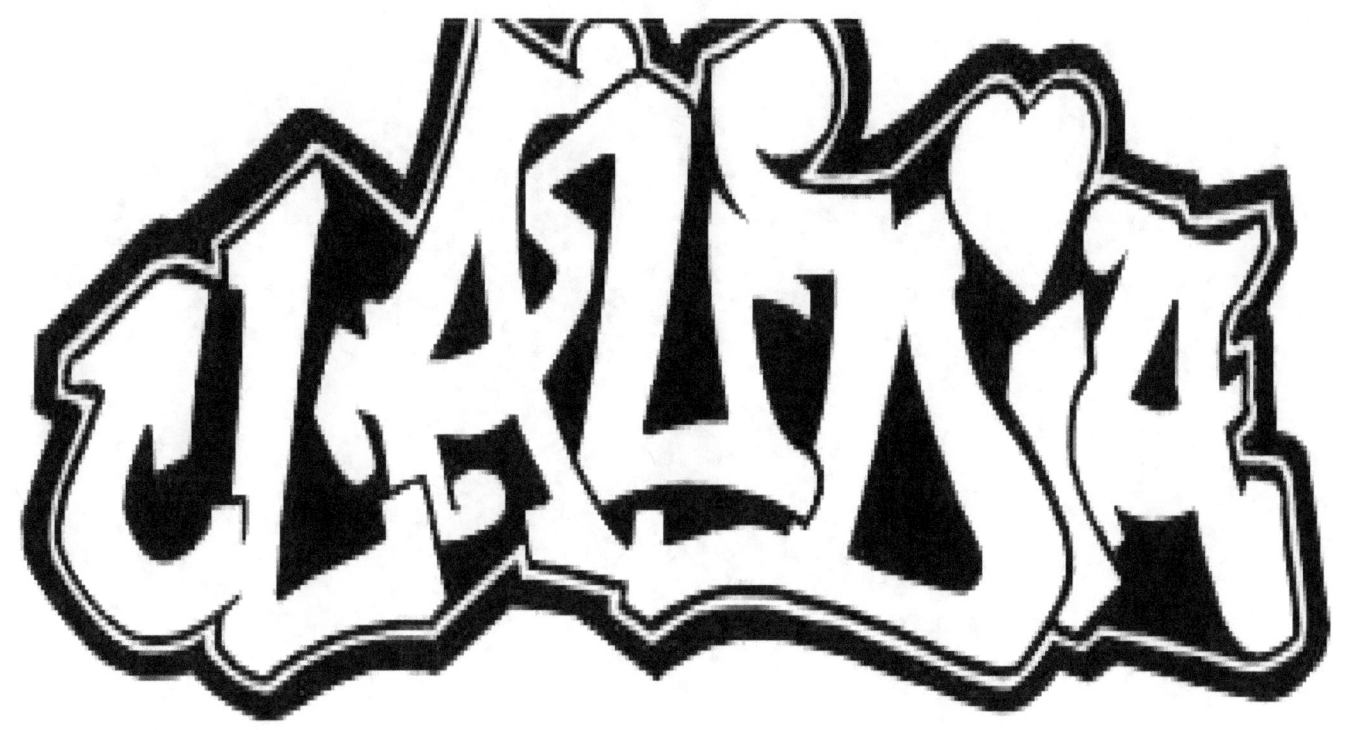

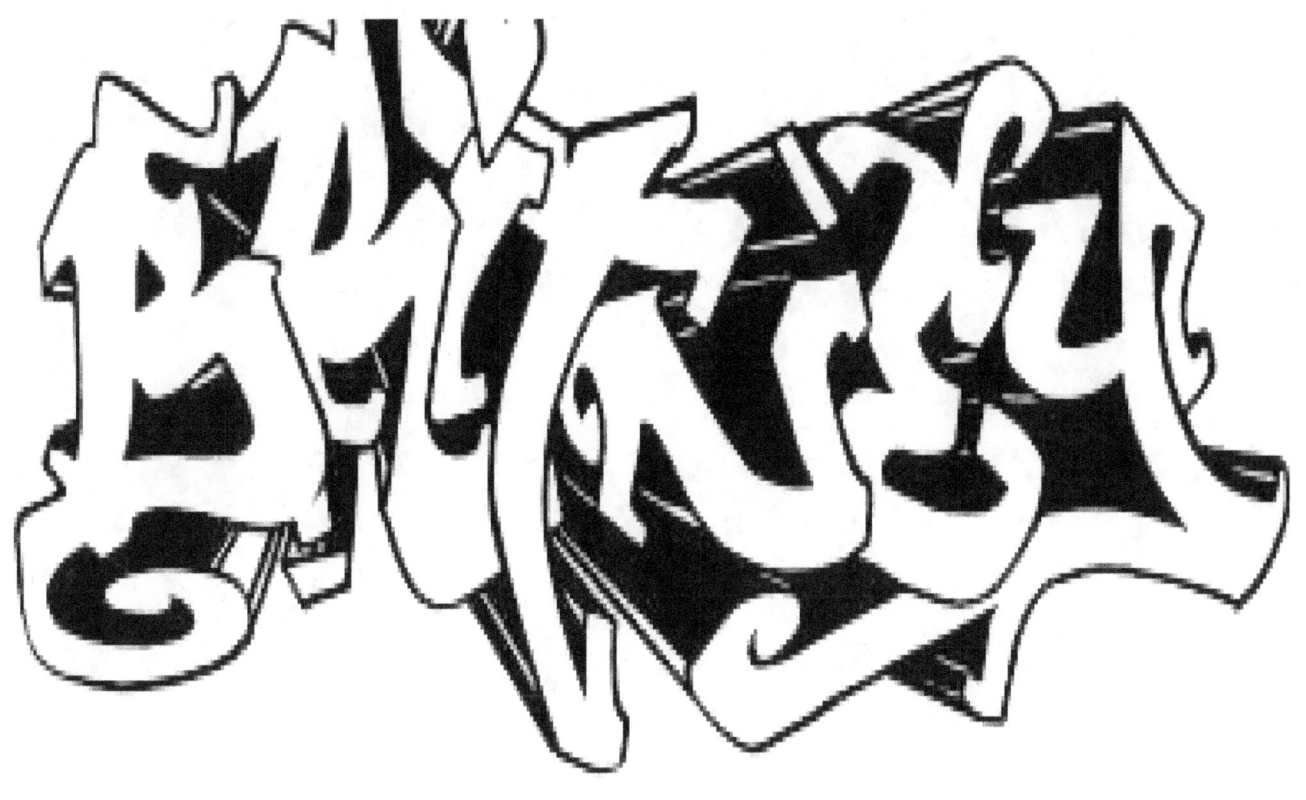

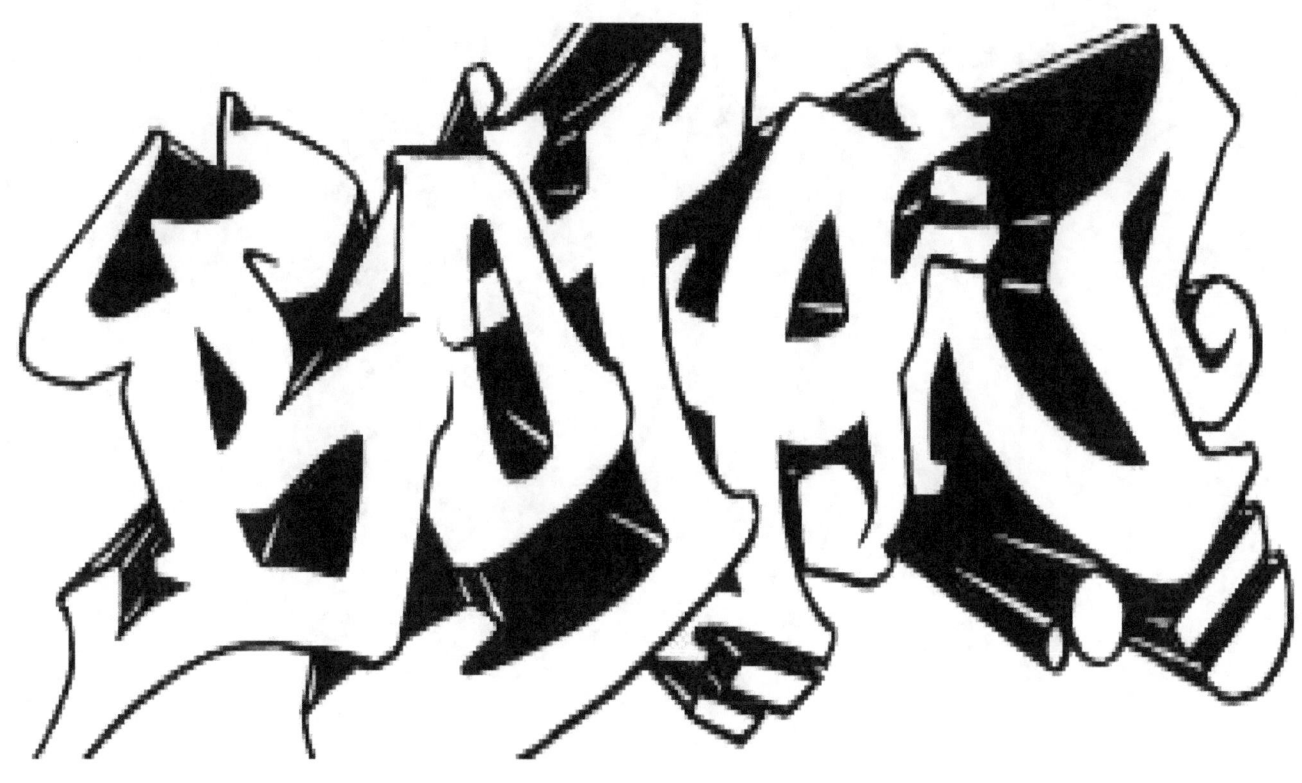

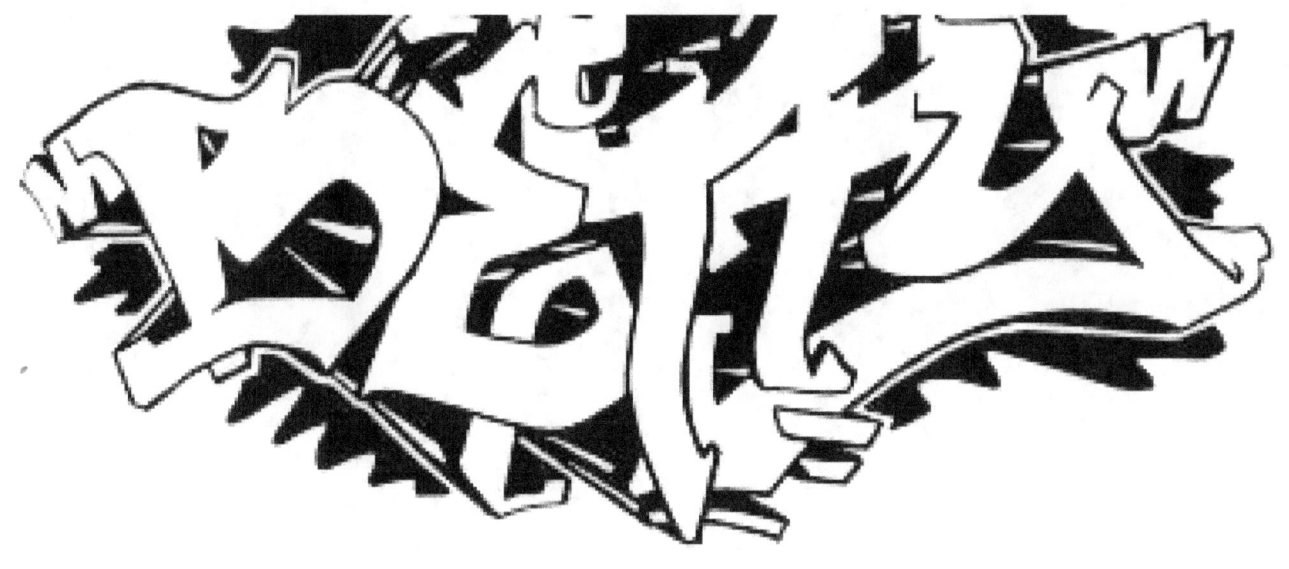

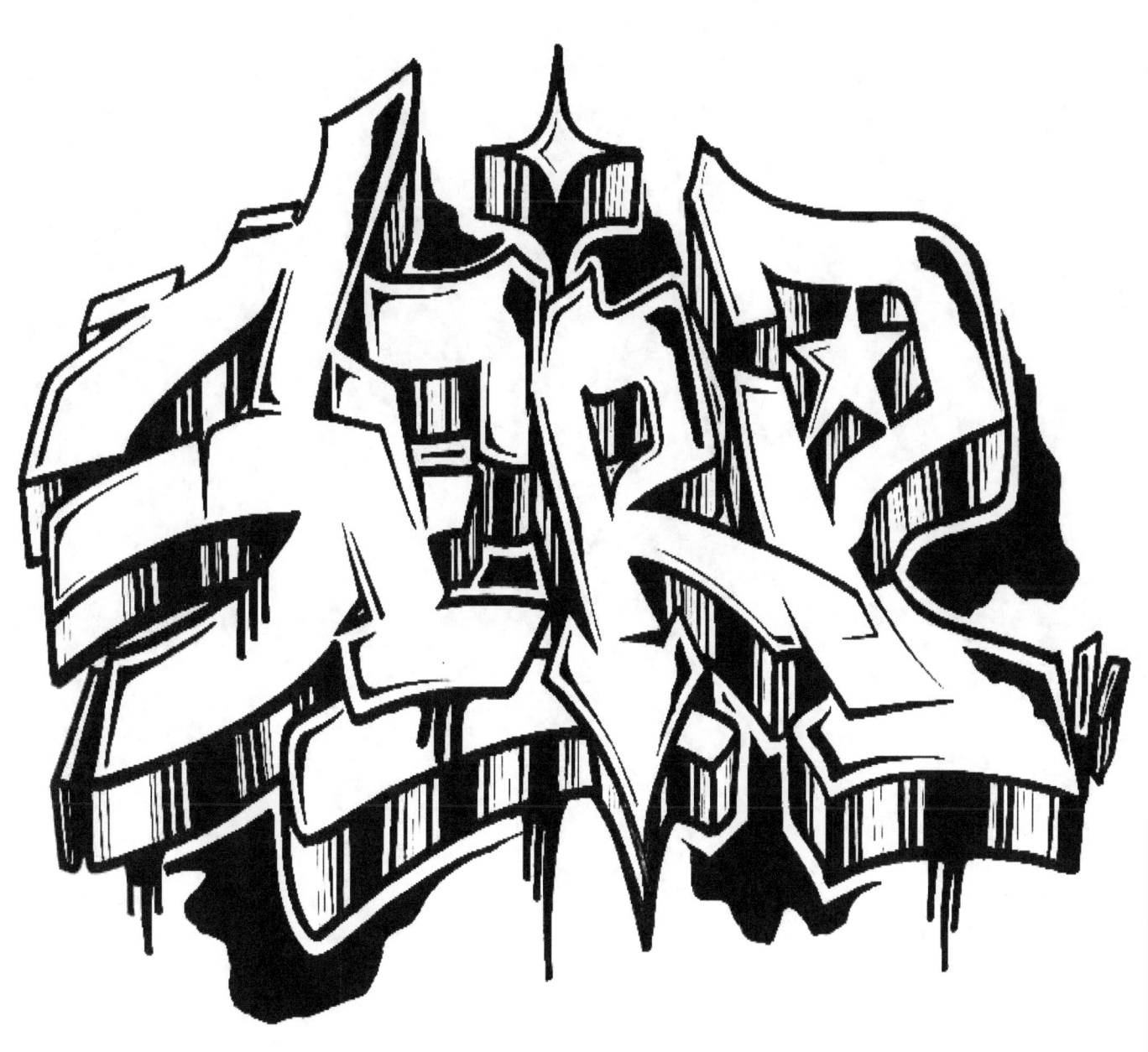

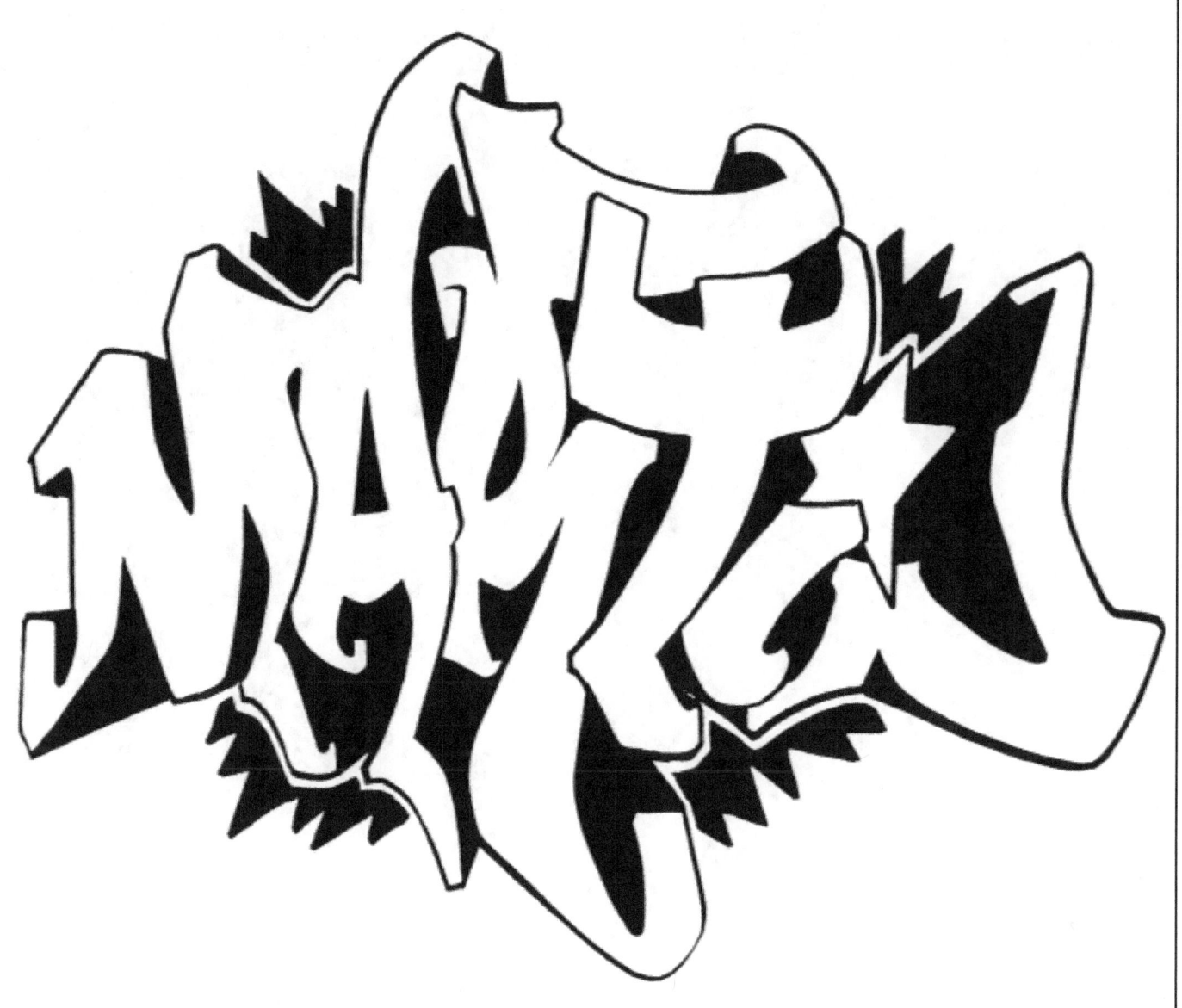

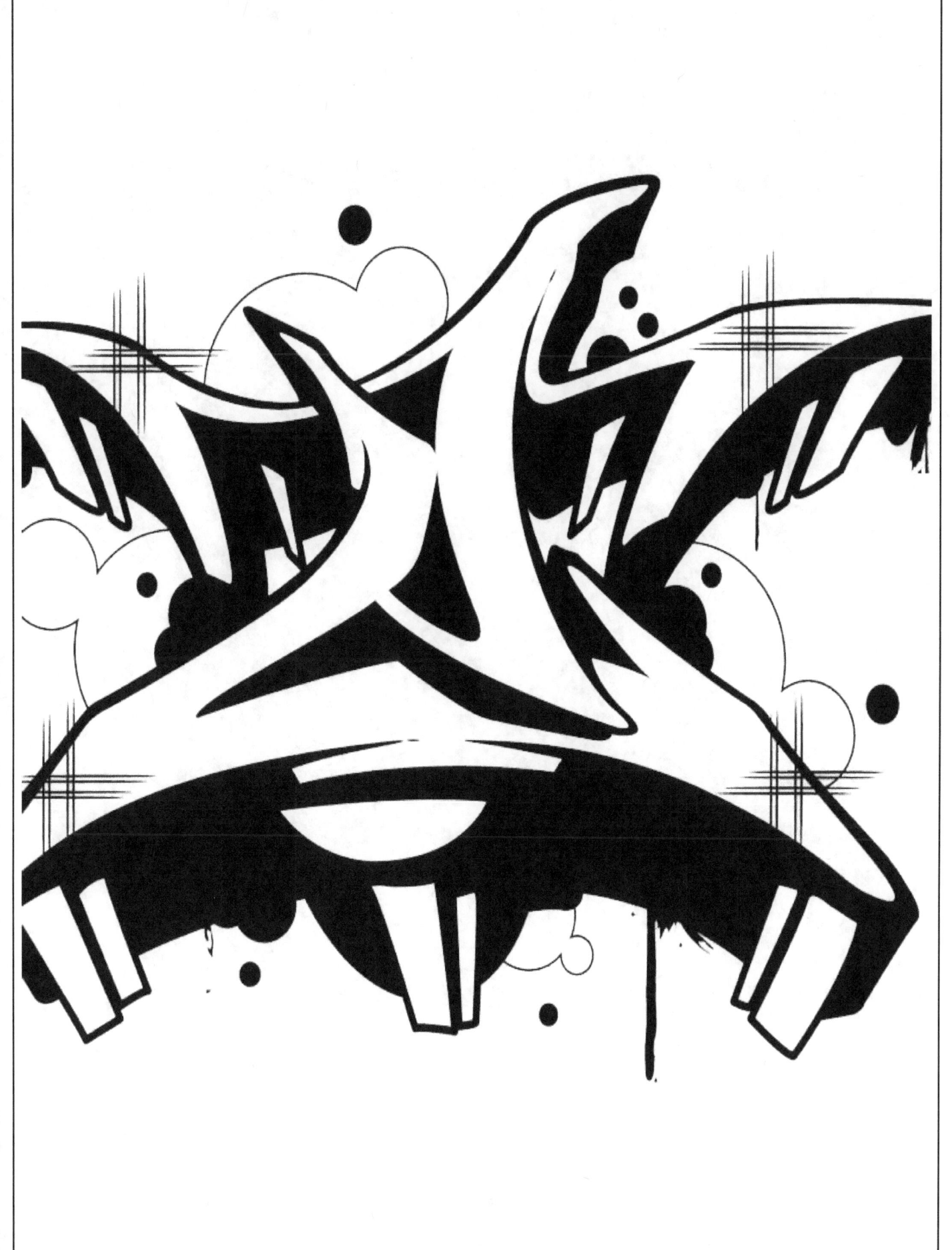

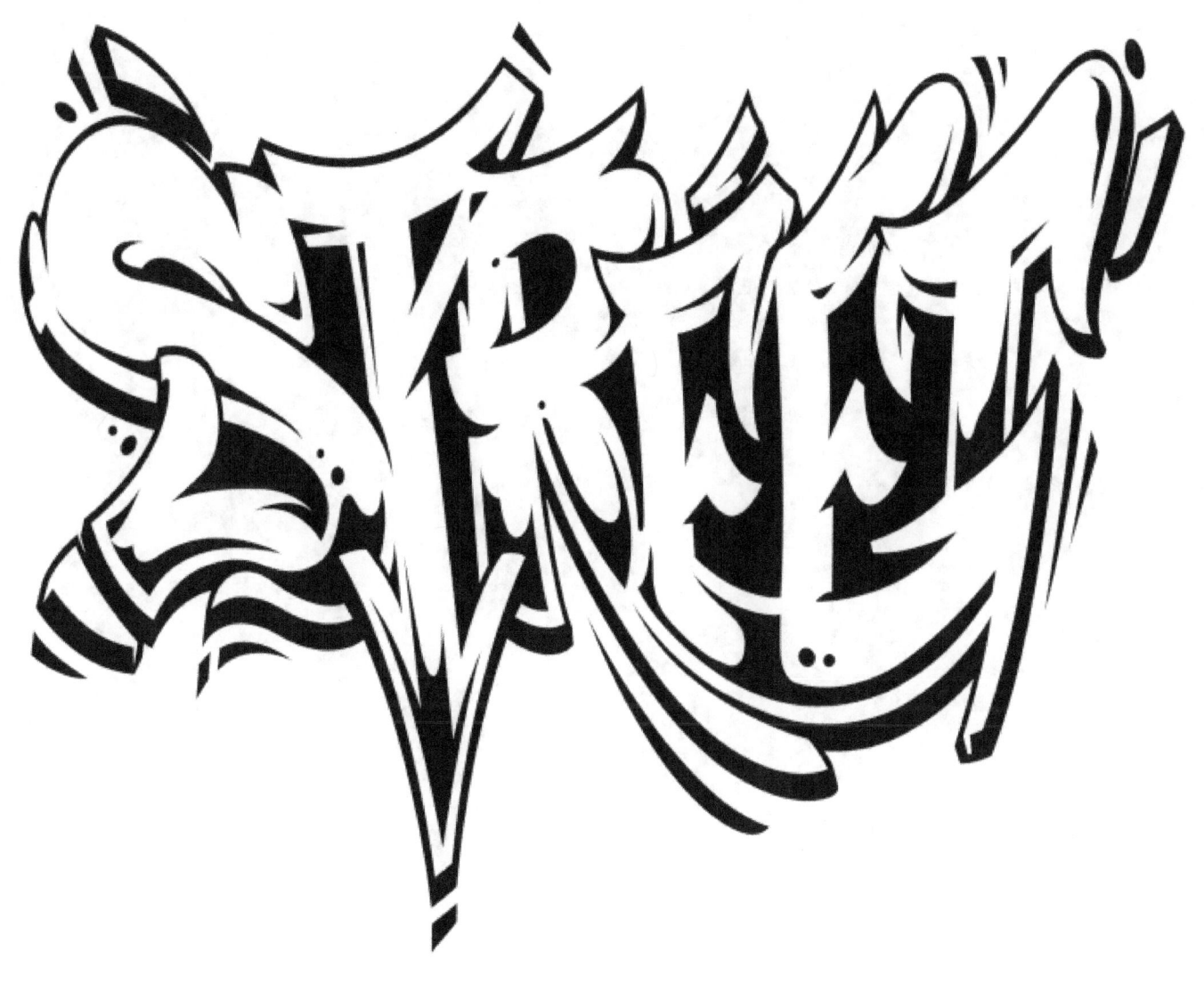

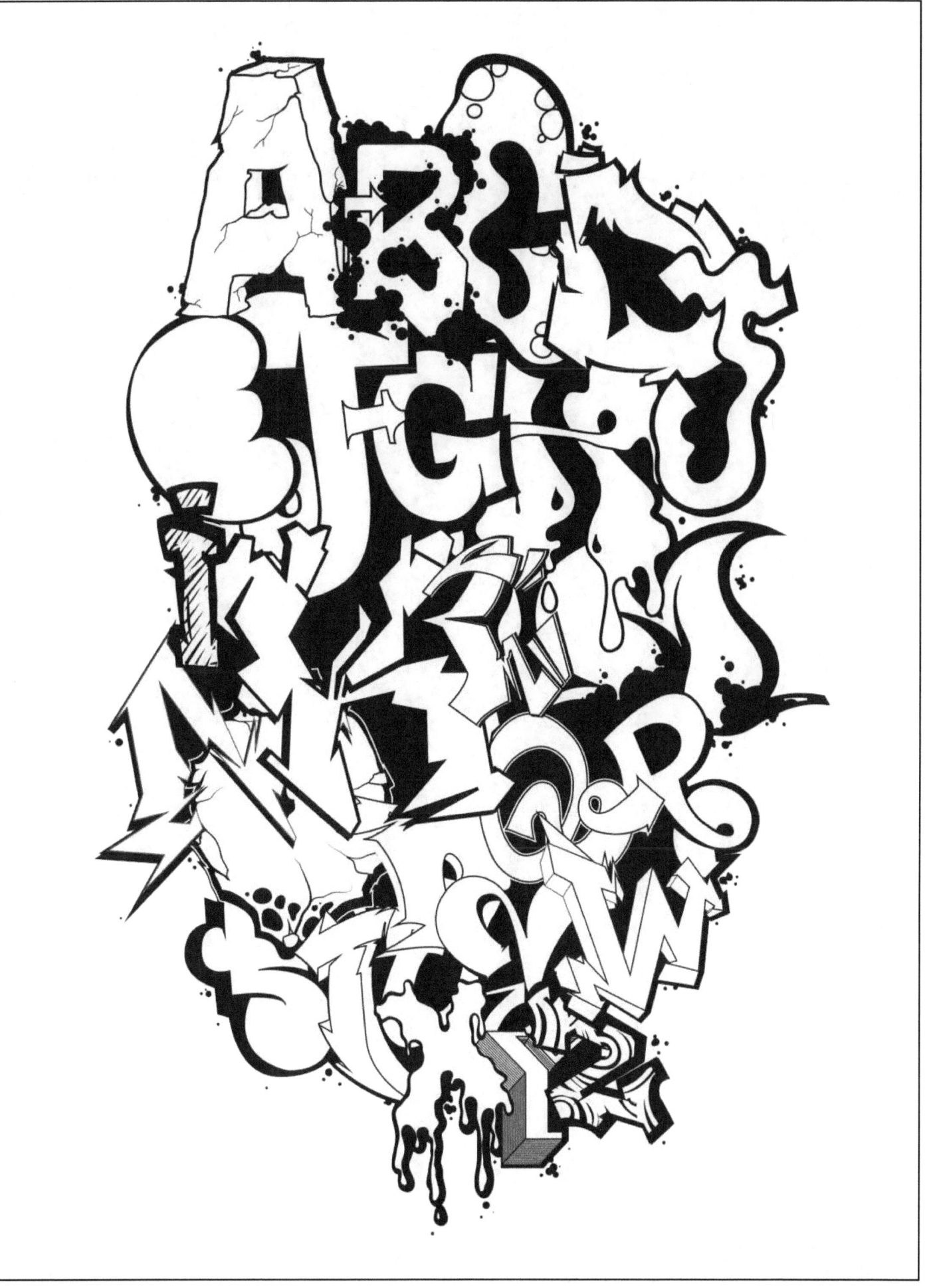

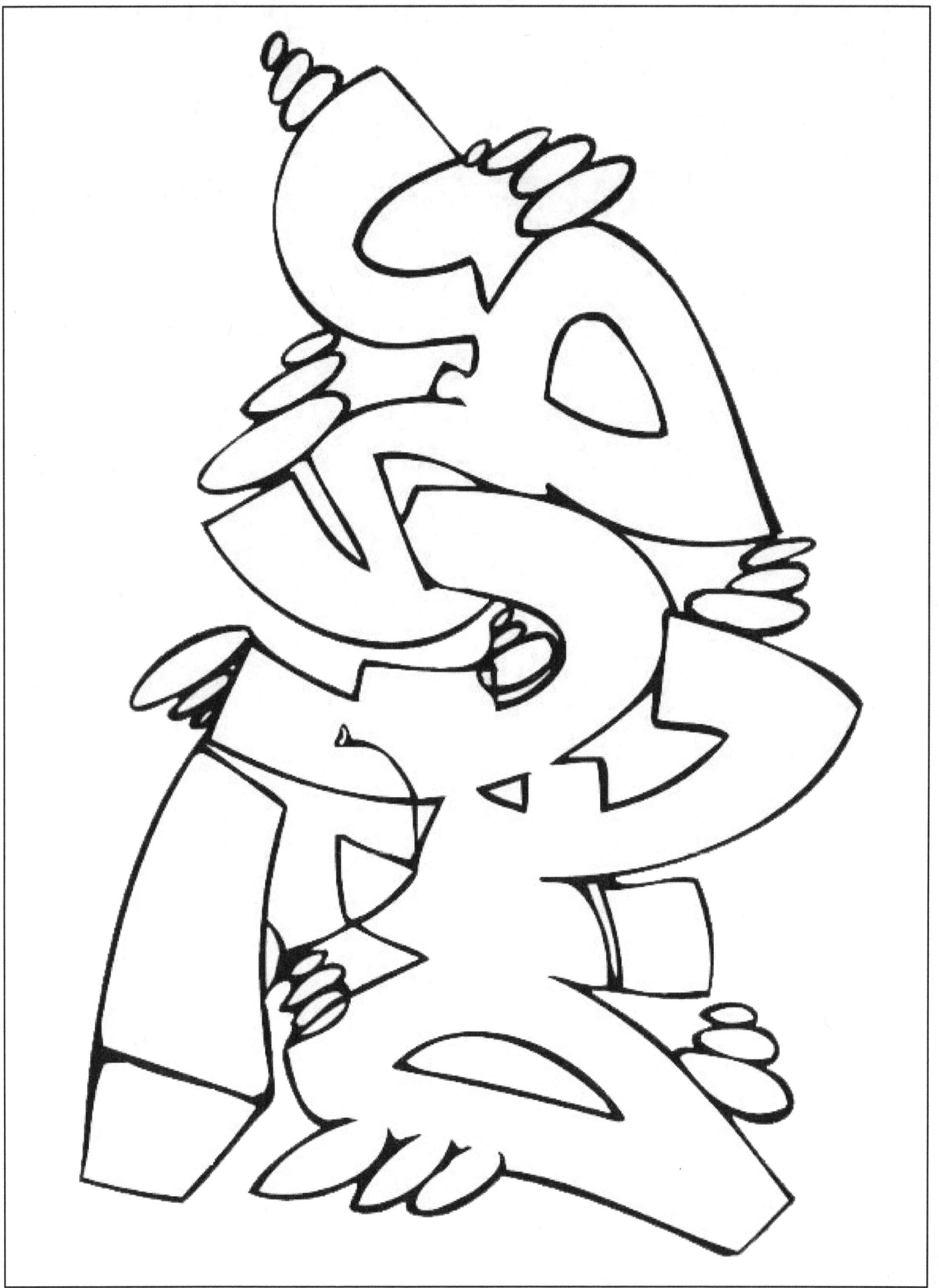

www.ingramcontent.com/pod-product-compliance
Lightning Source LLC
Chambersburg PA
CBHW081002220526

45467CB00008B/2663

* 9 7 9 8 7 1 6 3 8 1 9 9 5 *